THE
FINAL
ANSWER

Grantland Rice   Michael Werboff

THE
FINAL
ANSWER
and other poems

BY

GRANTLAND RICE

SELECTED AND WITH A FOREWORD BY

John Kieran

A. S. BARNES and COMPANY

NEW YORK

FOREWORD

GRANTLAND RICE gave his heart and his life to the writing of sports but above and beyond that, and often at the top of one of his famous sports columns, he put his soul in verse. He loved poets and poetry. He reveled in rhymes. Keats and Shelley, Tennyson and Swinburne, Housman and Masefield were his heroes. Kipling was his idol. He often borrowed the verse forms and the rhyme schemes of his favorites for sportive purposes, to brighten a dull day, perhaps, or add lustre to a stirring story. Much of this was ephemeral. It touched on the topic of the day and its significance vanished overnight. But there were other days when the verses atop the column dealt with the things that were close to the heart and deep in the soul of Grantland Rice. These were too good to be lost in yesterday's—or yesteryear's—newspaper. They have been reclaimed here. In them the reader will find what Keats said was all that we needed to know on earth—Beauty and Truth. They vary in mood, tone and tempo but they join in revealing the whole man that was Grantland Rice—athlete, sportswriter, philosopher, soldier, poet, husband, father and the finest friend any of us shall ever know. Making these selections was a labor of love and a great joy because going through the dusty clippings brought back myriad memories of happy days with a man who did more than anyone else to make them so for all around him. At his death it could have been written of him as his idol, Kipling, wrote of another:

E'en as he trod that day to God, so walked he from his birth,
In simpleness and gentleness and honor and clean mirth.

Grantland Rice lies buried in Woodlawn Cemetery in New York City. He still lives in the hearts of his friends and in the verse in this book.

JOHN KIERAN

BY WAY OF EXPLANATION

These are the rhymes from forty years
Of service on a thousand fields.
Rhymes gathered in from fame and tears,
From broken dreams and roaring cheers,
From flaming swords and shattered shields.

These are the lines that come to one
From blood and roses—dreams and pain;
From hammered bodies in the sun
To winners storming wind and rain.
A medley from the bugle call
And moonlight on the garden wall.

These are the rhymes for friends I've known,
Through shine and shadow—up and down.
For those who knew time's gilded throne
To derelicts, from farm and town.
But where they move along Time's chart
The final port is still the heart.

CONTENTS

[ix]

NONE BUT THE BRAVE

WHEN THE GAME IS DONE

THE
FINAL
ANSWER

THE FINAL ANSWER

This is the word I bring you, from jungle and from town,
From city street where weary feet are seeking vague renown,
From cotton fields to northern snows, or where the west winds cry,
This is the word I bring you: "Keep strong, or else you die."

They speak of battle's finish—they talk of peace to come.
They cheer for songs supplanting the bugle and the drum.
They think of dreams in clover, beneath a cloudless sky,
Remember what I tell you: "Keep strong, or else you die."

Peace on this war-torn planet? I want it understood
I like a cheerful neighbor—but give me hardihood.
Give me the fiber needed to face what lies ahead,
To make good for the living, to make up for the dead.

The easy road is over, for in this swarming hive
Those who can take a beating are those who will survive.
We've ripped a pleasant planet, it's too late now to sigh.
Remember what I've told you: "Keep strong, or else you die."

COURAGE
and
INSPIRATION

THE CONQUEROR

I am the conqueror of clown and king
Of prince and pauper in this shaking world.
I rule the race, as to the field I bring
Power that leaves so many banners furled.

I grip the young and old, and drive them back
From heights they might have gained, except for me.
I am the ghost that haunts each open track
By vale or mountain or by plain and sea.

I am the barrier that wrecks a dream.
I am the fog from which the cautious steer.
I take from life its color and its gleam.
I am the master—and my name is Fear.

UPHILL—AND ON

O, sons of men, whose goal is dust,
Where raw Fate waits at bay,
Whose life is parry, whirl and thrust,
And soon the blade is brown with rust,
Its scabbard thrown away;
O, sons of men, above all things
There must be courage thrown
Against the crashing storm that swings,
Against red bolts the lightning flings
Where each must stand alone.

O, sons of men, the night is long
That closes out our wars,
Though now and then life has a song,
The battle still is to the strong
Who have no fear of scars;
There must be courage, or the thrill
Of life's forever fled,
The broken and the beaten fill
All roads that lead from vale to hill,
Where blood was less than red.

The book of life is full of pain,
Of heartache and of hurt—
The road is dark through wind and rain,
We stumble where the dead have lain
Beneath the dreamless dirt;
The goal of dreams is faint and far
Beneath the heavy pack,
And scar must follow after scar,
But, sons of men, the shining star
Of courage lights the track.

THE UNAFRAID

Unlock the door upon Time's ancient vaults
And you will find this record in the rust,
That life is full of virtues and of faults
That melt and mingle in the age-old dust;
But there is still one shining light that throws
Its guiding beacon to the vast parade—
A shining light that glitters, gleams and glows—
I lift my glass and drink—The Unafraid!

This life knows one great scourge—and that is fear;
Defeat and loneliness—poverty and pain,
The crash of dreams, when coming night is near,
Or haunting shadows that surround the brain—
The fist of Fate that falls upon the soul—
Where, here and there, a few, still undismayed,
Look through the flame of battle to the goal—
I lift my glass and drink—The Unafraid!

This is no world of softness, dreams and ease,
But greed and hate and sin and endless strife;
Where baffled humans sail the storm-swept seas
To find somewhere the Holy Grail of life—
The Holy Grail of Courage—facing odds,
Taking the game, just as the game is played,
Unbeaten by the Fates—the breaks—the gods—
I lift my glass and drink—The Unafraid!

BEYOND THE STORM

I, who have seen the storm ride down the sky,
Heavy with ghosts and shadows and dead dreams,
Still see one ray of light that will not die,
One star that gleams.

This is the star called Courage that must shine
If the old world we know may hold its place
In the vast march of planets, line on line,
Through endless space.

The star that shines above the midnight gate,
Brighter in darkness than in noonday's glare,
Beyond the puny reach of hostile fate,
Or time's despair.

If this star fades, where men in broken pride
Slink from the battered trench, or quit the helm,
Then what we call our world should swing aside
For some new realm.

THE GIFT OF THE GODS

If I may call you friend, I wish you this—
No gentle destiny throughout the years,
No soft content, or ease, or unearned bliss
Bereft of heartache where no sorrow nears—
But rather, rugged trouble for a mate
To mold your soul against the coming blight,
To train you for the ruthless whip of Fate
And build your heart up for the bitter fight.

If I may call you friend, here's to the flame
That burns you into truer, stouter steel—
Here's to the savage struggle of the game
That rips and hammers, as you sway and reel,
Until at last you stand on shattered ground,
Feet firm upon the blood-stained sod below,
Laughing at fear, through all the storms around,
Roughshod and ready for the next hard blow.

If I may call you friend, I wish this, too,
As you grope blindly out the narrow beat,
That you may have one old-time dream come true,
Which is one more than most men ever meet;
That you will hold this worthy as a prize
For all the traps with which the course is lined,
Not scorning it with too ambitious eyes
That look for something you can never find.

AS WE GROW OLDER

No one knows where the road may take us
Out from the Inn, as the curtain falls.
No one knows where the barque of Charon
Points its prow when the darkness calls.
Facing the fogs with a dream to guide us,
Stumbling on to a grave new-made,
Take this thought to your souls, my brothers,
Nothing strikes at the unafraid.

What if the sunset's drawing nearer?
What if the shadows gather in
Thick with the ghosts of the mates who've headed
Into space where the comets spin?
Eyes to the front, though the mists are heavy,
Life at best is a brief parade;
Keep one dream in your hearts, my brothers,
Nothing shatters the unafraid.

HOW TO GROW OLD

If only through my heart there flows
A tide of spring, blue days and gold,
To match the gray of winter snows
That gather when the year is old—
A breath from morning that I knew
Before the twilight's purple thrust
Across the hills when night is due
And fields are faint with starry dust.

What if the drifting years slip by
In grim parade along time's chart,
Or ghosts of winter blur the sky
If April lingers in the heart?
If one can march through fog and haze
To see the sunlight on the hill
And feel through winter's shadowed days
That spring is calling to him still?

Though age may come in with the tide
And thinning hair, perhaps, is gray,
Young April whistles at my side,
A careless vagabond at play;

I'll take him with me for a mate
And make him share the growing load
Until we pass the final gate
That opens on another road.

Young April—with its ghosts of dreams,
With all the glory of the game—
I hear again the singing streams
And see the dogwood in its flame;
The years may pass in quick review
But this is all I care to know—
The sun is gold—the sky is blue—
And dogwood lanes are white with snow.

THE GREAT BOATMAN

Charon, the day is fading—night is near
Where the last darkness closes out each dream,
And I shall come to meet you without fear
To face the shadows of your silent stream.

Why should we ask you what may wait beyond
Amid the myriad ghosts who drift and roam,
Since each freed soul must be a vagabond
Cut off from ancient ties of hearth and home?

You offer all there is from time and space,
Eternal years—the last red star of night,
Yours is the great adventure of the race
That no small earth can match with human flight.

No paltry march of days to find some shore
Where golden dreams of love and beauty call,
No seven seas to limit steam and oar,
Or wings that fly and droop before they fall.

What other boatman points his barque of flame
By moon and sun and planets, faint and far?
Where sorrow, heartache, struggle, wealth and **fame**
Are lost amid the thrills from star to star?

ONLY THE BRAVE

Who are the brave? I've asked this, deep in doubt.
The ones who laugh at death, and take their chance?
Or those who know what life means, those in doubt,
Lost to all dreams of glory and romance?
Who take the bitter road that leads nowhere
To slog along—to challenge—and to dare?

Only the brave know what the hunted are—
The battered—and the shattered—and the lost—
Who know the meaning of each deep, red scar,
For which they paid the heartache and the cost.
Who've left the depths against unmeasured odds
To ask no quarter from the ruling gods.

Born—live—and die—cradle along to grave.
The march is on—by bugle and by drum—
Where only those who beat life are the brave—
Who laugh at fate and face what is to come,
Knowing how swiftly all the years roll by,
Where dawn and sunset blend in one brief sky.

TO THE LAST OF ALL

"Cowards die many times before their deaths;
The valiant never taste of death but once."

—SHAKESPEARE

Whether it's Heaven—or whether it's Hell—
Or whether it's merely sleep;
Or whether it's Something in Between
Where ghosts of the half-gods creep,—

Since it comes but once—and it comes to all—
On the one fixed, certain date—
Why drink of the dregs till the Cup arrives
On the gray date set by Fate?

Is life so dear—are dreams so sure?
Are love and strife so strong,
That one should shrink from the fated step
To a road that is new and long?

The soul—the grave—and the after-trail—
The Mystic River's flow—
How have the living earned their guess
Where only the dead may know?

Who is there left to raise a hand
And send his will to God,
That he should live where others know
The song of spade and clod?

One by one till the line has passed—
The gutter-born—and the crown—
So what is a day—or a year or two—
Since the answer's written down?

What is a day to a million years
When the last winds sound their call?
So here's to the days that rest between—
And here's to the last of all.

THE ROAD ISN'T LONG

There's always one answer to sob or to song—
The road isn't long;
Tomorrow—tomorrow—tomorrow—and then
The sunset is over in one flaming thrust;
The deep twilight fades into darkness again
Where the hurt and the heartache find covering dust;
And the dreams that we knew
Are gray ghosts that gather where darkness is deep,
To haunt us no more all the far ages through,
As we find the last solace of silence and sleep.
The fogs and the mists shroud the sigh and the song,
But the road isn't long.

The breaks may be right or the breaks may be wrong—
But the road isn't long;
The sunrise is shining a moment or two—
The storm flames are flashing where lightning rides high—

We fall and we rise till the finish is due
By the bank of the river where Charon floats by;
For all it's a fight—
The battle front winds by the path each must know,
The tears blend with laughter—and weakness with might—
Where gray Fate is pointing the way we must go—
The pace may be set by the swift and the strong—
But the road isn't long.

OUT OF THE DARKNESS

There must be courage when you seek the light
Through the deep darkness that may wait ahead;
There must be faith in finishing a fight
That no defeat can ever leave for dead;
There must be in your argosy one dream
That you can follow, though the road is long,
By storm and shadow through the dawn's first gleam—
And there must be a song.

There must be courage, or the road is lost
Through the gray fogs that hold our march at bay;
There must be courage, as we pay the cost
That Fate collects along the right of way;
Battered and broken as we slog on by,
Seeking the light beyond the mists that throng,
There still must be one dream that will not die—
And there must be a song.

THANKSGIVING EVE

Thanks for the little and the simpler things
    That only average fellows ever know,
The few breaks, now and then, that rough fate brings
    To scatter sunlight over winter's snow.
The grip of hand—a quick smile, here and there,
    A friend or two along roads rough and crude,
And more than all in facing life's despair
    Thanks for the golden gift of fortitude.

A DREAM OF THANKSGIVING

There's an old house in a clearing where the smoke winds thin and
blue
Over pines that bend and whisper, where the low winds rustle
through,
And I hear them calling to me from the fragrance of the loam:
"Don't you know that it's Thanksgiving and you ought to be at
home?"

There are ghosts beneath the maple trees, and one of them is mine;
There are shadows in the clearing beneath the whispering pine
Of the kids that romped together underneath a friendly sky
As they waited for the turkey and the berries and the pie.

There are phantoms in the orchard as the ancient door swings out,
Where a mother's voice is calling and is answered with a shout,
Where the little circle gathered for the feast that waited then,
Through the golden days that vanished and will never come again.

And now from far and far away, beyond the shadows cast,
I hear again lost voices from a day forever past;
Where from the stubble by the lane the larks sang, clear and keen,
The reveille of morning when the world was young and clean.

From far away we saw the lights and followed, you and I;
From far away we heard the drums and left a friendly sky;
And now we whisper through the streets or from a lonely den:
"God grant we haven't lost the road that leads us back again!"

For the pallid faces haunt us in a land of strife and fears,
As their weary feet go marching down the hopeless length of years;
Where above the sullen murmur and the traffic's endless roar
We can hear lost voices calling from the morning lanes once more.

Where we still turn to the fragrance of the harvest and the loam,
Where we hear the bluebirds singing in the golden air of home,
Or the pine trees bend and whisper as the low winds rustle through
By an old house in the clearing where the smoke winds, thin and blue.

So we'll give our thanks together for the dream by land and sea
Of the shadows in the clearing from a day that used to be;
Of an old Thanksgiving morning that has followed down the years
Where the pallid faces haunt us in a land of strife and fears.

BRING ME A SONG

Out from the darkness that gathers around,
Here, where the road is long,
Out from the shadows where phantoms are found
Bring me a brave, young song—
Bring me a song to the heart of December
Where the dim sun is cast,
Bring me a song that I can remember
When the last dream is past.

Out from the sighs and the sorrows and tears,
Born of the drifting throng,
Out from the heartache and hurt of the years,
Bring me a brave, true song—
Bring me a song to this fading December
Where the faint light is spread,
Bring me a song that I can remember
When the last faith is dead.

Out from the battle of greed and of hate
In the clash of the weak and strong,
Out from the bitterness sent us by Fate,
Bring me a brave, clear song—
Bring me a song to the gray of December,
Turning the world to gold,
Bring me a song that I will remember
When the last love is cold.

REVERIE

When spring comes back, old dreams come, too,
Across the starlight and the dew,
From vanished years and distant ways
Through many, many yesterdays;
Dreams that in winter's sweep of snow
We thought had passed forever by,
But when the Southwind whispers low
And April's blue gets in the sky,
When bud and bloom crown lane and hill
We find them waiting for us still.

Sometimes they seek us in the breath
Of lilac bush along the lane;
Sometimes they bring back life from death
Through some old song—some dim refrain—
Or yet—a rosebud in the rain
Will beckon to our startled gaze
And back again by vanished ways
We thread lost twilights to the blue
Of life's lost morning that we knew
In some far blossom-scented spring
Where gypsy hearts went wandering.

And then, they come to us and wait
At April dusk beside the gate,
And from the drifting shadows there
They weave a well-remembered face—
A red rose gathered in her hair—
A smile that sweeps through time and space—
And in the whisper of the trees
A voice drifts back upon the breeze,
As tender and as low and sweet
As winds that ripple through the wheat
And stir again old memories.

CHRISTMAS EVE

I was sitting alone in the fading light
That came from the yule log's glow,
Under the berries of scarlet and white
Where time had taken an ancient flight,
And my head was nodding low.
When far away, as a dream is born,
I heard the call of the Little Tin Horn.

I heard the call of the Little Tin Horn
And the shout from a merry band,
And I saw the cows come out of the corn,
On the day that a golden dream was born,
And the sheep from the meadowlands.
And out where the eerie shadows creep
There were Little Boy Blue and Little Bo Peep.

I couldn't believe it—but it was true,
For into this golden dream
There came the Old Woman Who Lived in a Shoe,
(She honestly didn't know what to do)
As I watched the yule log gleam.
And Little Miss Muffet and Little Jack Horner
Were whispering in a near-by corner.

Little Bo Peep you have lost your sheep
But I have lost my way
Through the gathering mists, where the shadows creep,
For the years are long and the night is deep,
Where lost ghosts stand at bay.
Little Bo Peep, won't you let me go
To the Christmas stocking I used to know?

And Little Boy Blue won't you lead me back
Through the endless years once more?
Will the Little Tin Horn find a vanished track
That will take me home where the night is black
To port on a long lost shore?
O Little Boy Blue, can I go with you
To a day that's young where a dream comes true?

THE LAST PORT

No matter how heavy the fogs,
How dark the night—
No matter how thorny the path,
For king or for clown,
Somewhere beyond there's a dawn
That is silver with light,
For those with a grip on some dream
No Fate can break down.

OF LATE YEARS

How long the Summer days were then—
How slow time moved upon its way,
When I was just a lad of ten
I thought each year had come to stay.

But now the fast years hurry by
At dizzy pace from sun to snow,
Like meteors against the sky
That flame and vanish as they go.

YESTERDAYS AND TOMORROWS

How far is yesterday from tomorrow?
As far as the rolling rivers run.
As far as joy can be from sorrow.
As far as the earth is from the sun.
Tomorrow's coming to bring the cost,
But yesterday is forever lost.
You'll find one thing in this weird existence,
That comes to all between land and sky.
No matter the sweep or the endless distance,
Youth is the one thing gold can't buy.
Not all of the wealth that the mines set free
Can buy you an hour that used to be.

ROAD TO THE FUTURE

Since human nature is the same,
  With all its well-known fluff,
Since Homer smote his bloomin' lyre
  And Vergil did his stuff,
And since we know that there will be
  Small change a thousand years from now,
Why bother with the sobbing note,
  Or eke the furrowed brow?

I'd like to sit and weep about
  The so-called human race,
Except I know how slow it's been
  Since Adam set the pace.
Just give us, say, five thousand years,
  Deep dipping in the past,
And maybe in five thousand years
  We'll find the road at last.

No one can knock its courage from
   The first and age-old span—
"The beauty of this wide green earth,
   The bravery of man"—
So let's not look discouraged to
   That far-off era when
The human race will trade its brains
   For horse sense now and then.

THE WAY OF IT

There are roads that lead through valleys where the grass is soft and
    green;
There are lanes that lead through morning where the friendly maples
    lean;
But for those who face the battle where the far height holds its thrill
The only goal worth finding
Where the rock-filled road is winding,
Where the heavy burden's binding,
Is the goal upon a hill.

We may think of life as something that is built up from a dream;
We may hear old songs that call us where the shafts of morning
    stream;
But the storms beyond are waiting for the raw, unconquered will,
And though hearts and hopes are breaking
As we come to bitter waking,
Yet the only road worth taking
Is the road that leads uphill.

NONE
but
THE BRAVE

SONGS ABOVE THE DUST

Where rain-wet crosses know the dawn that gleams,
Safe from the crashing shell, the raw steel's thrust,
They face the resurrection of their dreams
Where only songs now live above their dust.

Songs of forgotten valor, where the storm
Of unleashed lightning hurled its dread barrage;
Songs of old shadows that again take form
In grim and silent waiting for the charge.

This is their recompense—the gray wind brings
Lost threnodies still vibrant with their fame,
And from the snow-clad uplands winter sings
Old songs they helped to write in blood and flame.

What mound of earth can keep their voices still?
What pressing coverlet of clay or clod
Can dim the deathless strains by plain or hill
Where Seeger sleeps and Brooke smiles up to God?

Their ghostly music lingers like the breath
Of summer when the harvest has its yield,
Before each knew his "rendezvous with Death,"
In "some far corner of a foreign field."

What hate or greed or cowardice can bar
The eerie, golden echoes that still creep
Where Kilmer waits beyond some flaming star
That lights the holy darkness of his sleep?

They sang their songs heroic with the fire
Of unstained courage through the shell-swept mud,
Up to the barricade of trench and wire
That knew the shining glory of their blood.

Let beauty light the world and hold its sway,
Let life and love drift by, twin souls of time,
Soft arms, and lips of roses, and the play
Of starlight eyes that give the world its rhyme.

Yet there is still a deeper glow that shines,
A deeper thrill that comes with bated breath,
As the faint dawn breaks through on waiting lines
And the blue steel means victory or death.

Shall their songs be forgotten with their dust?
Songs which their valor wrote by hill and glen?
Sing, winds, above their rifles, red with rust!
Blow, bugles, soft and low, blow Taps again!

PAGING ALL POETS

"They had no poet, and they died."
—ALEXANDER POPE

Kipling, we have missed you in the world we know today—
Missed your Fuzzy-Wuzzy and your Road to Mandalay;
Missed your Tommy Atkins and the brave songs that you sung,
When the world was saner and a few of us were young.

Kipling, from Valhalla, can't you send me back your pen,
So I can sing the glory of MacArthur and his men?
So I can tell the story, where the flames of Luzon burned,
And send on to eternity the fame that he has earned?

There is need of ships and planes but when the strong meet strong,
All fighting men, who look on death, can always use a song—
A song that knocks against the heart, that rips into the soul,
A song that helps to carry men beyond the bitter goal.

Old Homer sang of Hector and Achilles in his time.
But, Homer, from your ancient dust I need a braver rhyme.
Send me from vanished centuries no one will know again
A golden epic tribute for MacArthur and his men.

I'm just a wayside poet—in this mighty ebb and flow,
Where the magic of MacArthur is beyond all words I know—
A miracle of heart and brains that calls, above the flood,
For a soul that's dipped in genius and a pen that's dipped in blood.

So, poets, from a thousand years, rise from your faded dust!
Bold Byron, Keats and Shelley, help to clean away my rust.
For above all lyrics written I must have a godlike pen
To pay a fitting tribute to MacArthur and his men.

COME ON, TEAM!

(A United States war cry heard by charging troops in Sicily.)

"Come on, Team!"—
Here were the words they knew, and understood,
The final answer to a captain's dream,
Suiting the moment and the fighting mood,
Brought in from other fields, and other days,
Part of their heritage in friendly grip,
A call far-echoed from remembered ways
That had no part of foxhole, tank or ship.

"Come on, Team!"—
This is their answer when the chips are down.
Where great bombs thunder or the red flares gleam,
By battered road or through some shattered town,
Part of their younger souls in younger years,
When it was one for all, and all for one,
Lifting them high above all doubts and fears
Until the game was over and the fight was won.

IN AN OLD ATTIC

There are his glove and bat and ball.
There is his football, with its score.
There is a sweater on the wall,
There are the cleated shoes he wore.
But far off, where they fight and die,
His plane patrols a distant sky.

Here is the room that held his dreams,
A pitcher, where the headlines glow,
A running back on winning teams,
Such dreams as only mothers know.
And somewhere, lost upon the air,
I hear the echo of a prayer.

SUMMER AND DEAD SOLDIERS

Lost winds from home have found us
    Through fields of poppy stain;
They whisper all around us
    Of lovers in the lane;
Of twilights far behind us
    That held June's ancient vow;
They brought old dreams to find us—
    As if it mattered now.

Our crosses lean together
    With each far wind that blows,
The same in summer weather
    As through the winter snows;
And no one may remember
    The snowdrift or the sun,
Where June and bleak December
    To us are always one.

Yes, summer crowns the mountains
    Where moonlight seeks the plains;
There's music in the fountains
    That leap to summer rains;
The dogwood blossoms scatter
    Their snowdrift through the glen—
For us it doesn't matter,
    And never will again.

For you the rose, entwining,
    May climb the garden wall;
For you soft eyes are shining
    Where summer dusk-winds call;
But what if June has found us
    Who may not even know
If poppies bloom around us,
    Or drifts of winter snow?

A BOW TO THE INFANTRY

Our airplanes fly through a blood-flecked sky and scatter their crates
    of death.
They guard the air where the comets flare and fight to the final death.
They sweep the way to the conquering day, but over the battle's din
In the swirl and reel there's the call for steel, as the infantry charges
    in.
When it's give and take for the goal at stake, when the main job
    must be done—

        It's the infantry that holds the bag,
        It's the infantry from vale to crag,
        It's the infantry that plants the flag
        When the gory field is won.

Through the seven seas by storm and breeze our Navy gives its best.
We rule the foam from Truk to Rome and leap to the killing test.
But the big day comes with the rolling drums when the dirty work
    is due,
When it's stab and slash in the closing crash, as the infantry charges
    through.
And who takes charge in the red barrage when it comes to the naked
    blade?

        It's the infantry that storms the hills,
        It's the infantry that thrusts and kills,
        It's the infantry that knows the thrills
        When it comes to the big parade.

Just count their ghosts from the vanished hosts since Alexander's
    rule—
In the primal plan it was man to man when it came to the winning
    school.
It's steel to steel on the racking wheel, since Cæsar's ancient day,
And it's still the same in the modern game where raw steel holds its
    sway.
Under red skies, with bloodshot eyes, who sends in the final thrust?

        It's the infantry that must rip through fate,
        The infantry where it is hate for hate,
        The infantry that must storm the gate
        From dust unto final dust.

THE FOURTH AND THE FLAG

Under its rippling rolls of red
With its wide, blue sweep spread overhead,
Over the living and over the dead,
Here's to the flag.
Back through the years where our fathers stood,
Stemming forever the charging flood,
Born in glory and bathed in blood,
Here's to the flag.

Thrown to the winds of the East and West,
To the North and South—in their spangles drest,
To the high and low—through the bitter test—
Here's to the flag.
One flag only for you and me,
By plain or mountain, by air or sea,
The heritage of our dream to be—
Here's to the flag.

By rain-wet crosses, by dune and wave,
By the ghosts from many a far-off grave,
It still stands guard for the dreamless brave,
So here's to the flag.
You from the farm or the nearby town,
From city streets—with your king or clown—
Where would you be if the flag came down?
Here's to the flag.

A MESSAGE
FROM A FRONT TRENCH

When my time comes and all farewells are said
    To what few friends may still survive the fight,
I shall not shrink to hear the ghostly tread
    That signals Death is stalking through the night
To lead me forth across the Mystic Moor
    Unto the Tavern of the Silent Land—
But I shall smile—and through the open door
    We two shall go, as good friends—hand in hand.

There I shall meet the friends who've gone before,
    And we shall gather in a room apart,
And, cup to cup, shall pledge the days of yore,
    Soul unto soul and silent heart to heart;
And there beneath the crimson rose that nods
    And sways above us, free from toil and strife,
We'll quaff to you—forgotten by the gods—
    Poor souls who linger at the Inn of Life.

COMES ONE WITH A SONG

"In the strife and the tumult that sweeps us along,
Comes one with a song"—
The song is now bl rred by the guns and the storms
That cover the wor ld as the battle line forms,
But in some day ahead, when we've buried our dead,
The song will return till the last candles burn
And the last tents are spread.

By land, sea and air in the test of the strong,
They still sing a song—
A song that still echoes from mountain to shore
Above the wild blasts of the big guns that roar—
The song of the free in a new world to be,
Where a new world is thrilled and the last guns are stilled
From green hillside to sea.

DISARMAMENT

I wonder what they think of, when gray ghosts get together,
The ones who fought to end all war and found the wooden cross?
Whose bodies hold the ground they won, unmindful of the weather,
Where rain and sun to them are one, beyond the touch of loss?

I wonder what their vote would be when, just as dusk is falling,
Their ghostly dreams go back again to lanes they knew of old?
Or out the path they hear again remembered voices calling
From those who come their way no more as time goes by untold?

Perhaps it doesn't matter now where, safe beyond all sorrow,
They hold their brave and simple rest bereft of haunting care,
Out where their ghosts can only see a golden, far to-morrow,
That waits beyond the twilight road where only dreamers fare.

Perhaps. But if they had the chance to see remembered faces,
To hear old voices calling them through autumn's hazy suns,
Or walk unbroken through the years amid old-fashioned places,
I wonder if their vote would be in favor of the guns?

THE TWO SIDES OF WAR

All wars are planned by older men
    In council rooms apart,
Who call for greater armament
    And map the battle chart.

But out along the shattered fields
    Where golden dreams turned gray,
How very young their faces were
    Where all the dead men lay.

Portly and solemn, in their pride
    The elders cast their vote
For this or that, or something else,
    That sounds the warlike note.

But where their sightless eyes stare out
    Beyond life's vanished joys,
I've noticed nearly all the dead
    Were hardly more than boys.

AIRBORNE

"Some flew east—some flew west—
Some flew over the cuckoo's nest."

—(OLD NURSERY RHYME)

Somewhere beyond the Southern Cross above the Seven Seas,
Along the bitter far-off roads, their pinions catch the breeze.
Their wings are black against the sky, by desert, surf and dune,
The ancient lullaby is lost against a rougher tune—

Some flew east—some flew west—
And some will fly no more;
Far, far out from the eagle's nest
Their mighty motors roar.
And wing by wing their rule will grow
Above all sea and sod,
Until they strike the final blow
For country and for God.

Faintly, I hear the old, old song when golden dreams were young.
But louder still I hear the wings where sudden death is flung.
Bravely the eagle rides the air, but in my fading dreams,
The dim, lost lullaby returns—how far away it seems—

Some fly east—and some fly west—
They take an endless track.
Through flame and steel they face the test
Around the world and back.
Their golden youth blots out the sky,
They let the comets plod,
As each one flies to live or die
For country and for God.

WHEN the GAME IS DONE

INVITATION

Get out your leather and sharpen your cleats,
What wants to bother with worry or strife?
Pan, the Mad Piper, is loose in the streets,
Filling our veins with the red wine of life.

Who cares for glory or money or fame?
I want to revel, to shout or to dance.
I want to play or to follow some game.
I want a grip on forgotten romance.

Come on, Mad Piper, and lead me astray.
I'm sick of cobwebs that clutter my brain.
Let's duck the path that is weary and gray,
Lead me, O lead me to April again.

THERE ARE A FEW LEFT

Who put the game above the score,
Who rate the battle as the test,
Who stand content, amid the roar,
Where they have given out their best;
No matter what the prize at stake,
Who prove that they can give—and take.

Who have no fear of some defeat,
No vain regrets to haunt their night,
Because the race went to the fleet,
Because the stronger won the fight;
Who do their stuff—win, lose or draw,
And laugh at Fate's inconstant law.

THE CALL OF THE UNBEATEN

We know how rough the road will be,
How heavy here the load will be,
We know about the barricades that wait along the track;
But we have set our soul ahead
Upon a certain goal ahead
And nothing left from hell to sky shall ever turn us back.

We know how brief all fame must be,
We know how crude the game must be,
We know how soon the cheering turns to jeering down the block;
But there's a deeper feeling here
That Fate can't scatter reeling here,
In knowing we have battled with the final ounce in stock.

We sing of no wild glory now,
Emblazoning some story now
Of mighty charges down the field beyond some guarded pit;
But humbler tasks befalling us,
Set duties that are calling us,
Where nothing left from hell to sky shall ever make us quit.

IT CAN HAPPEN THIS WAY

He took his turn, half-heartedly, outlining an excuse.
He figured he was beaten—so he couldn't see the use.
But when he made his little play, it took a lucky swerve,
A sudden, unexpected hop—a title-winning curve—
And straightway they exclaimed about his "courage" and his "nerve."

He started in with bulldog jaw to make a winning fight.
He started in to see it through, as any stalwart might.
But when he cut in with his play, it took a hard luck bound,
And caromed as it shouldn't have on any sort of ground,
And so they rose and branded him a "quitter" and a "hound."

Yes, courage is a fancy word that gives us all a brace,
And yellow is another term we splash about the place.
But there are things behind the scenes that none of us can see,
An edict from the gods of chance, whoever they may be,
Who set the score—and laugh aloud at our philosophy.

TO SPORT AND SPRING

When I am old, as years are measured,
When winter's snow is on my head,
And all the golden dreams I've treasured,
Like winter leaves, are brown and dead;
Though I am lost to nimble dancing
Where light-toed feet still hold their fling,
Old age can't wither all romancing
Where I can turn to sport—and spring.

With eyes, perhaps, that see but dimly
The younger generations leap,
That may not see at dusk how grimly
The long, gray twilight shadows creep,
Though gray and bent I still will follow
The flight of youth on silver wing;
By track and field, by hill and hollow,
I'll know the lure of sport and spring.

When one is close to youth and playtime
The passing years may take no toll,
And one can find that dreams of Maytime
Shut out life's winter from the soul.
What if old age from off the byway
Paints shadows on December's chart?
Where sport and spring call out the highway,
Eternal April holds the heart.

A SPORTING EPITAPH

Write this above my dust—in some lost grave.
"Here lies no hero—listed with the brave.
He had no thought of glory or of fame.
Beyond the score—he only loved the game.
And when the bell gave out its ringing call,
He had not much to give—but gave it all."

ALUMNUS FOOTBALL

Bill Jones had been the shining star upon his college team.
His tackling was ferocious and his bucking was a dream.
When husky William took the ball beneath his brawny arm
They had two extra men to ring the ambulance alarm.

Bill hit the line and ran the ends like some mad bull amuck.
The other team would shiver when they saw him start to buck.
And when some rival tackler tried to block his dashing pace,
On waking up, he'd ask, "Who drove that truck across my face?"

Bill had the speed—Bill had the weight—Bill never bucked in vain;
From goal to goal he whizzed along while fragments strewed the plain,
And there had been a standing bet, which no one tried to call,
That he could make his distance through a ten-foot granite wall.

When he wound up his college course each student's heart was sore.
They wept to think bull-throated Bill would sock the line no more.
Not so with William—in his dreams he saw the Field of Fame,
Where he would buck to glory in the swirl of Life's big game.

Sweet are the dreams of college life, before our faith is nicked—
The world is but a cherry tree that's waiting to be picked;
The world is but an open road—until we find, one day,
How far away the goal posts are that called us to the play.

So, with the sheepskin tucked beneath his arm in football style,
Bill put on steam and dashed into the thickest of the pile;
With eyes ablaze he sprinted where the laureled highway led—
When Bill woke up his scalp hung loose and knots adorned his head.

He tried to run the ends of life, but with rib-crushing toss
A rent collector tackled him and threw him for a loss.
And when he switched his course again and dashed into the line
The massive Guard named Failure did a toddle on his spine.

Bill tried to punt out of the rut, but ere he turned the trick
Right Tackle Competition scuttled through and blocked the kick.
And when he tackled at Success in one long, vicious prod
The Fullback Disappointment steered his features in the sod.

Bill was no quitter, so he tried a buck in higher gear,
But Left Guard Envy broke it up and stood him on his ear.
Whereat he aimed a forward pass, but in a vicious bound
Big Center Greed slipped through a hole and slammed him to the
    ground.

But one day, when across the Field of Fame the goal seemed dim,
The wise old coach, Experience, came up and spoke to him.
"Oh Boy," he said, "the main point now before you win your bout
Is keep on bucking Failure till you've worn the piker out!

"And, kid, cut out this fancy stuff—go in there, low and hard;
Just keep your eye upon the ball and plug on, yard by yard,
And more than all, when you are thrown or tumbled with a crack,
Don't sit there whining—hustle up and keep on coming back;

"Keep coming back with all you've got, without an alibi,
If Competition trips you up or lands upon your eye,
Until at last above the din you hear this sentence spilled:
'We might as well let this bird through before we all get killed.'

"You'll find the road is long and rough, with soft spots far apart,
Where only those can make the grade who have the Uphill Heart.
And when they stop you with a thud or halt you with a crack,
Let Courage call the signals as you keep on coming back.

"Keep coming back, and though the world may romp across your
        spine,
Let every game's end find you still upon the battling line;
For when the One Great Scorer comes to mark against your name,
He writes—not that you won or lost—but how you played the Game."

BALLAD OF THE GAMEFISH

"Only the gamefish swims upstream."
—COL. JOHN TROTWOOD MOORE

Where the puddle is shallow, the weakfish stay
    To drift along with the current's flow;
To take the tide as it moves each day
    With the idle ripples that come and go;
With a shrinking fear of the gales that blow
    By distant coasts where the Great Ports gleam;
Where the far heights call through the silver glow,
    "Only the gamefish swims upstream."

Where the shore is waiting, the minnows play,
    Borne by the current's undertow;
Drifting, fluttering on their way,
    Bound by a fate that has willed it so;
In the tree-flung shadows they never know
    How far they have come from the old, brave dream;
Where the wild gales call from the peaks of snow,
    "Only the gamefish swims upstream."

Where the tide rolls down in a flash of spray
  And strikes with the might of a bitter foe,
The shrimp and the sponge are held at bay
  Where the dusk winds call and the sun sinks low;
They call it Fate in their endless woe
  As they shrink in fear when the wild hawks scream
From the crags and crests where the great thorns grow,
  "Only the gamefish swims upstream."

Held with the current the Fates bestow,
  The driftwood moves to a sluggish theme,
Nor heeds the call which the Far Isles throw,
  "Only the gamefish swims upstream."

BEYOND ALL THINGS

"He played the game"—
What finer epitaph can stand?
Or who can earn a fairer fame
When Time at last has called his hand?
Regardless of the mocking roar,
Regardless of the final score,
To fight it out, raw blow for blow,
Until your time has come to go
On out beyond all praise or blame,
Beyond the twilight's purple glow,
Where Fate can write against your name
This closing line for friend or foe:
"He played the game."

"He played the game"—
What more is there that one can say?
What other word might add acclaim
To this lone phrase that rules the fray?
Regardless of the breaks of chance,
Regardless of all circumstance,
To rise above the whims of Fate,
Where dreams at times are desolate,
Where failure seems your final aim
And disappointment is your mate,
Where Life can write in words of flame
This closing line above the gate:
"He played the game."

THE DUFFER'S EPITAPH

(WITH A NOD TO R. L. S.)

Under the wide and starry sky
Dig the pit, and let me lie.
Gladly I've lived—and gladly die,
Far from this world of strife.

These be the lines you grave for me,
"Here he lies where he wants to be,
Here he lies by the nineteenth tee,
Where he's lied all through his life."

THE SHOCK

(FROM "THE REVERY OF AN UMPIRE,"
WITH APOLOGIES TO BEN KING'S "GHOST.")

If I should die to-night,
    And as with folded arms in death I lay,
Arrayed in shrouds of linen pure and white,
    Some rooter should bend over me and say,
"Old boy, I'm sorry that you're down and out;
I hope you'll get to heaven, for you're square;
I've seen you umpire many a hard-fought bout
Without one bum decision, I can swear—"

If he said that,
    Although my soul was even then a spook,
I'd rise at once in my large, white cravat,
    To get one look at him, one final look;
I'd make him pass me out that dope once more,
    The same quaint words that he had used before.
Yes, I'd rise up till he was done, and then—
    I'd drop back dead again.

THE WINNERS

Those only win who reach the gate
Through surf and storm and bitter gale,
Through pain and loneliness and hate,
Through all the sullen thrusts of Fate,
With battered prow and shattered sail,
Who look on life and death as one,
Until the closing race is run.

Those only win who see the goal
Beyond the baffling fog and mist,
Whose names are written on the scroll
Of those who stand with unbowed soul
Amid the thin, immortal list,
Who drive through fear and doubt and sin
Until the darkness closes in.

This is no life for soul or heart
That breaks or falters at defeat;
The weak are beaten at the start,
And only those who play their part
May face the rough and rocky beat;
The road is long—the dream is gone—
The fighting heart still carries on.

THE RECORD

When the Game is Done
   And the Players creep
One by one
   To the League of Sleep—
Deep in the Night
   They may not know
The way of the fight,
   The fate of the foe,
And the cheer that passed
   From applauding bands
Is stilled at last—
   But the Record stands.

The base hits made,
   And the errors wrought;
How the Game was played—
   How the fight was fought—
Though the Game be done
   Where the Night is deep

And one by one
    From the Field they creep—
Their day has passed
    Through the Twilight Gates,
But the Scroll is cast
    And the Record waits.

PREDESTINED

I am the ghost that follows men—I give each one his break,
For life is largely accident, no matter what they say—
I lift and lower at my will—I give and then I take—
And laugh to see the experts squirm and figure out the play.

In some I plant the yellow streak, which they must hold from birth;
To some I bring a fighting heart, which holds the world at bay;
To millions I bring tragedy—to millions I bring mirth,
But only those I give the breaks can have the right of way.

I let an able artist starve—I take a dolt of brawn
And give him fame and wealth to spare—the laurel on his brow—
And I have followed this set plan from time's first streak of dawn,
And I will keep this schedule up a million years from now.

A SPORTING PHILOSOPHY

Let's keep trying to win;
Let's keep playing the game;
Let's keep trying to spin
The whirligig top called fame.
But isn't there something more—
This life we know isn't long—
Something beyond the score?
So let's keep room for a song.

There is the dawn and the moon;
There is the flaming glow;
But here is the sunset soon—
Sooner than you may know.
What do we get out of life
Picking the right and the wrong?
Weariness, hatred and strife—
So let's keep room for a song.

SUNSET

and

EVENING STAR

THE MAGIC PIPER

Now that Young April's back again
Where Spring has melted out the snow,
Why should we tarry longer here
Who have so far to go?

The walled-in streets—the sodden crowds,
What can they offer in their blend
To dogwood blossoms down some lane
Or roads that never end?

The ghosts of glory—phantom fame,
The tawdry baubles that we prize—
What are they to the hills that call—
The blue in April skies?

Why should we tarry longer now
To find where deeper pleasures dwell?
Since life can show but these two things—
A hail—and a farewell.

A SONG TO APRIL

I have loved you, April, for the blue mist in your eyes,
For the sunlight's yellow gold that lingers in your hair,
For the sudden tears that start, when in hurt surprise
You turn back to rain and mist as if you didn't care;
For the wild plum blossoms I have seen against your breast,
For the music in your throat that sings from hill to sea.
For your whisper through the crowds that brings a wild unrest,
All the golden memories of youth that used to be.

I have loved you, April, for the dreams that still return
When you dance across the hills and call me from the snow,
Dreams that come to me again from new-lit flames that burn
In a heart that turned to you, long and long ago.
Dreams of moonlight through the trees and roses on the wall,
Where the stars in southern skies across the night are strung,
All the vanished yesterdays that I can still recall
When the dogwood blooms again and all the world is young.

There are lanes that wind again where youth and youth go by,
Hand in hand and heart to heart through all the golden day,
Where the apple blossoms shine against a sunset sky—
There is nothing else that counts around the world away.

Fame and wealth and greed and gain, leave them to the old;
I would rather turn again and find the road to spring
Where young Pan is piping in a glen of green and gold
And young April's waiting with another song to sing.

I am coming, April, to the tryst that we have known
Where the fields are green again and the sky is blue;
There is moonlight down the walk where old dreams are blown
From the happy country where a dream can still come true.
Though the gray is in my hair, look into my heart;
You will see the boy of old where the dogwood gleams,
Singing down the road again as the years depart,
On his way to Romany, to roses and to dreams.

MAY MADNESS

Romany—Romany—I have heard you calling,
Romany—Romany—though I'm growing gray,
I must go and look again at the sunlight falling
On the dogwood by some stream, near the close of day.

When I was a younger man, all I knew was battle,
Thunder from the crowded stands, at the winning score;
I still like the crash and smash, where the jarred bones rattle,
But I've found some other turns that suit me even more.

Romany—Romany—there's a wind that's drifting
Out beyond the Seven Seas, where the jungles wait;
I can only dream of them, where the light is lifting
Just a straying step or two outside the city's gate.

I have dreamed, as others have, of the far-off places,
Winding from Nairobi on across the Khyber Pass;
South Sea isles and Congo streams and painted savage faces,
All the roads that lead beyond the city's sweating mass.

Romany—Romany—I was so mistaken—
I have seen the dogwood buds blossom nearer home;
I have watched the rolling surf—blue and white and shaken,
As it brought me dreams again on a nearer foam.

While the crowds are roaring still at the crashing thunder
Of the rally and the drive that stirs the souls of men,
Can you blame me if I wait to see the magic wonder
Of the sunset on the oaks when May comes back again?

THE MONTH OF ALL

You may take your winters southward,
You may have your golden Junes,
You may have your summer mountains
Or your eastern fog-swept dunes;
But I'll take the first red ember,
Where the Painter works his will,
When it's morning in September,
Or it's noon-day in September,
Or it's twilight in September,
And the flame is on the hill.

There is orange down the valley,
There is crimson out the lane;
There's a fleck of purple tinting
Where the maples meet the rain.
For the glow that I remember,
With an everlasting thrill,
Is a morning in September,
Or a noon-time in September,
Or a twilight in September,
When the flame is on the hill.

OCTOBER

I've watched the colors creeping
In all their golden glow.
I've watched the crimson sweeping
Along the lanes I know.
I've marked the first red fleck on
The green of yesterday;
The scarlet patches beckon,
And who am I to stay?

My fragile will goes under
Within the city's fold,
When I think of the wonder
That hills and valleys hold.
Let others seek the smartest,
The richest at their ease;
I'd rather meet the artist
Who paints the maple trees.

THE LUCKY ONES

Once more their camp smoke, clear and true
Goes up to meet the sky;
Once more they sound the moose call
Where the river rushes by;
And you, and I, and one or two
Who know what we have missed
Can only think in envy of
Their far October tryst.

The crowds are thick along the streets
Where through the weary day
Their wistful faces seem to dream
Of something far away;
Of lucky ones who see at dawn
With all its purple blend
A trail that leads through silent woods
Beyond the river's bend.

A FEW SIGNS

There's a north wind faintly calling, as the first dead leaves are falling,
Of a stretch of wooded country and our camp smoke, thin and blue;
And it speaks of quiet places, league on league from pallid faces,
Where the underbrush is silent till the big moose crashes through.

All my life gray fate has found me with the dizzy crowds around me,
Through the stadiums and subways ever wearily I tramp.
But when north winds come to woo me there's a call that whispers
    to me
Of a solitude that beckons to the glory of the camp.

And at times along the low bank, far beneath the mountain's snow
    bank,
There are trout scales from a breakfast that no chef might ever know;
With the scent of bacon frying and the first ducks southward flying
From the bitter snarl of winter to a softer land below.

And though desk and den may bind me, in my dreams at least you'll
    find me
Where the far pines bend and whisper and the moss and lichen grow.
And perhaps I'll slip the tether, with a few good mates together,
Who will let the old world amble any way it wants to.

FROM THE OPEN

Wind-tanned and sun-tanned, down the crowded street,
Mingling with the millions in the drift of restless feet.
Looking on with startled eyes, as one might read a book,
Watching anxious faces with their weary, haunted look.

I could see him looking on in a sort of daze,
Thinking of the open leagues through uncharted ways,
Turning to the quiet hills, holding all his dreams,
Where the moose and caribou seek the forest streams.

I could see him shake his head, as he wondered why
Men should run in crowded packs, where the walls are high.
Huddled into beaten throngs, broken in by fate,
With the open world outside, just beyond the gate.

CLOSE
to the
HEART

WHEN I AM DUST

(To Kate)

When I am dust, at night above my sleep
The winds will stop and sing one song that's true;
A song remembered, though the dark is deep,
And I will stir and dream—and dream of you.

The winds will whisper and my dust will hear
And see lost moonlight on a garden wall,
And I will find again a vanished year
We knew together, where old echoes call.

There will be flame again where ashes were,
With blood of roses poured into my heart
That beats again, where pulses wake and stir,
And hand will reach for hand, too far apart.

And I will see the darkness turn to gold,
Hearing your voice, that sounds like singing streams,
Not knowing I am dust, nor graves are cold,
Nor that a ghost walks with you in his dreams.

VOICES OF THE NIGHT

Last night you called from some forgotten year;
You spoke to me across the wall of night;
Or was it but the wind that echoed near
And whispered to me as it wheeled in flight?
Wind of the night from pathways we had known
Before the journey called me forth alone?
I know not—only that last night, as then,
I heard your voice again.

Last night you sang to me—the old song crept
From out the years and life's forgotten ways;
Or was it that the tavern music swept
My heart and soul on back to other days?
That carried me from out the night of fears
Into the light of life's all golden years?
I know not—only that last night—as then—
I heard you sing again.

Last night you came to me and brought me rest
From care and strife as in the days of yore;
Or was it but the ashes of dead roses pressed
Between the leaves I turned to see once more?
Ashes of roses from the days of gleam
When life was more than ashes of a dream?
I know not—only that last night—as then—
You came to me again.

ABOVE THE DARKNESS

(To Florence, My Daughter)

Deep in the dusk, Dear, the roses are sleeping;
Down from the hills, Dear, the low wind comes creeping,
Creeping and whispering
"Dreamer—good-night—
Dream of the morning
And God's world of light—
Dream—O Little One—dreams that are true,
Dreams of the starlight, the dawn and the dew,
Safe in your nest, Dear,
Sleep, Dear, and rest, Dear,
God in His heaven keeps watch over you."

Over the world, Dear, the twilight is falling,
Low through the dusk, Dear, the south wind comes calling—
Calling and whispering
"God give you rest—
God in His goodness
Keep guard by your nest;
Dream—O Little One—dream of the light,
Dream of the morning that He shall kiss white—
For while you sleep, Dear,
His care shall creep, Dear,
From the far skies to your cradle tonight."

TO A FRIEND

Others have given you gifts worth the keeping,
All that I have is a song;
All that I have from the sowing and reaping,
Just a thin melody, lilting and leaping,
Blown from the dust where the twilight comes creeping
Where you may wander along;
Thrown to the winds where the open road gleams,
Made up of nothing but star dust and dreams.

Others have given you things to remember,
All that I have is a song;
Gray as the shadow-strung fields of November,
Dull as the glow of a slow-burning ember,
Thin as the first falling snows of December
Sent to you out of the throng;
Only a wandering, lyrical wraith,
Made up of nothing but friendship and faith.

VIA CHARON,
THE ANCIENT BOATMAN

(To Frank Condon, Ring Lardner, Don Marquis, Odd
McIntyre, George Daley, Bill McGeehan, Bill Mac-
beth, Eddie Neil, Bill McNutt and others of the old
guard who recently have beaten us to the border.)

There are too many gaps in the ranks I knew
When the ranks I knew were young.
When the roll is called, there are still too few
Who answer "Here!" when the call is due—
There are too many songs unsung.
But Charon's boat is a busy barque—
And the dock gets closer as dusk grows dark.

Pilot—who looks to your river trade
Where the shadowy Styx rolls by
You've taken your pick for the mystic glade,
Lardner—McGeehan—and Hammond's shade
Drifts through a starless sky—
And somewhere—deep in the reedy tarn—
Boze Bulger is spinning another yarn.

Charon—answer me this today—
From all of the world's corrals,
Why do you always look *my* way?
I'm not worried about *your* play—
But why do you pick my pals?
From the Inn we knew where the flagons foam,
One by one you have called them home.

One by one, on a mist-blown eve
Wearing your ghostly hood,
I've seen you plucking them by the sleeve,
Telling them each it was time to leave,
Just as the show got good.
With a lifted glass, as I looked about,
I've seen them leave as the tide rolled out.

Charon—I'm sorry I failed the test—
You're not the one to blame—
You picked the brightest—you picked the best—
You carried them off to a dreamless rest
That towers above all fame.
Don—Odd—Percy—and Bill and Ring—
No wonder the angels soar and sing!

Listen, Pilot, the last of all
Who knows where the journey ends—
When you have come to the final call
Where the candle flutters against the wall,
Kindly forget my friends.
For friends are all that a little earth
Has yet to give that has any worth.

Fame and Gold? They are less than dust—
Less than an April song—
They are less than weeds in the earth's dull crust
When a friendly hand in your own is thrust
And an old mate comes along.
But dock lights flame with a sudden flare—
And Charon beckons—and who is there?

The Flame of the Inn is dim tonight—
Too many vacant chairs—
The sun has lost too much of its light—
Too many songs have taken flight—
Too many ghosts on the stairs—
Charon—here's to you—as man to man—
I wish I could pick 'em the way you can.

A MARINE COMES HOME

(THE BODY OF LIEUTENANT JOHN W. OVERTON, OF
YALE, THE MARINES AND TENNESSEE, KILLED IN AC-
TION JULY, 1918, COMES AGAIN TO THE HOME PORT.)

There is but silence now—and the dark night—
Where once he found the glory of the game,
And knew the golden glamour of the fight
With its brief moment of exalted fame;
There is but honor—and the quiet dust—
Where still the flaming torch rides out the years
Above the battered helmet's gathered rust
And the blurred mist of Sorrow's falling tears.

He has come home again to find old dreams
Beneath the shelter of his native sky,
By friendly hills, lost lanes and singing streams
Where winds, blown out of morning, rustle by
To whisper to him through the guarding pines
That cast deep shadows down the silent glen,
Or call to him through spring's new blossomed vines:
"The guns are still—and you are home again."

One summer morning on the Soissons road,
Leading his men at more than daring pace—
And then the spirit seeks a new abode
To find its freedom in eternal space;

Here the great runner fell, as he had starred,
In other days when he had worn the Blue,
Always in front, until with body scarred,
He sent his soul to see the last charge through.

We ponder for a moment, then forget;
Life rushes by above the fading dust;
New dawns break through, new suns in splendor set,
And yet the helmet with its growing rust,
The automatic and the service cross,
The tattered khaki that we once acclaimed
Pay silent tribute to a nation's loss,
Earth-covered ashes where a brave heart flamed.

There is but silence now—and darkness deep—
Where once gay youth walked by with lifted head;
There is but honor—and the rose-crowned sleep
That death sends only to its valiant dead;
There is but honor—is there more to ask
Where one is safely by the last alarms?
When each has finished with his given task
To find the Mighty Mother's guarding arms?

OVER THE BORDER

(To those who have gone before)

You have taken your travelers' cloaks from the inn, where only the top
    belong;
The music is low and the candles are dim, and there is a lull in song;
And those who are left lift a silent glass to the gaps that none may
    fill—
"To a fairer field and a better game—to a goal with a greater thrill."

The song will start and the candles gleam, for the game must still go
    on—
But we stop and turn as we look around for the friends who have
    passed and gone;
For a friendly hail and a friendly grip, in the room where the lights
    once burned—
But the travelers' cloaks are off the rack, where an empty cup is
    turned.

All that we bring to the inn is this—the travelers' cloak we wear,
All that we take from the inn is this—wherever the road may fare;
All that we get from the inn is this—the friends that we know are
    true,
Shoulder to shoulder and blood to blood—till the call of the road
    comes through.

What new road does the rover fear, when some one knocks at the inn,
And leads the way to an untrod trail, as far as the comets spin?
On with the travelers' cloak again, as we call from the restless throng,
"Good luck, old friend, till we find the way that leads to another
    song."

GEORGE ADE

The Hoosier's left us—so the world today
Has lost a share of sweetness and of light,
And there is now so little left to say
When such old friends fade into waiting night,
Except the memories that come from time,
So far beyond our feeble prose or rhyme.

The Hoosier's left us—where the outer rim
Has claimed another from our waning pack.
One of our best to see the candle's dim
And wavering glow fade out along life's track.
You set your star of glory in time's sky—
Friend for so many years—good night—good-by.

NOW YOU CAN WEEP, MY LADY

(A FEW LINES TO IRVIN COBB OF PADUCAH, KY.)

There's a shadow on the blue grass where the light has left the sky
And the mourning meadows echo to the south wind's saddened sigh.
The gold of all the sunshine in Kentucky's turned to gray.
O, you can weep, my lady; O, you can weep today.

Yet he would not have you weeping where Kentucky's winds drift by,
Who in his golden giving never gave the world a sigh.
He is home in old Paducah, where they miss his laugh today,
But the sweetest flowers of the South will hide his heart away.

REX BEACH

There is so little any one can write
When one has left who leaves a void so great.
There is so little left to morning's light,
Or noonday sun, or sunsets at the gate.
There is no place for tears in deeper grief
That brings a heartache that is past belief.

There should be something that can take the place
Of his firm handclasp and his winning smile.
There should be something in life's killing pace
To bring lost dreams to some dim afterwhile,
Where one can meet a friend again and know
That ghosts still walk beyond the twilight glow.

But there is now a fairer place ahead
Where those of us who knew him well shall meet
Together, with the others that are dead,
Part of a happy band where each can greet
The one we've missed—beyond the last good-by,
Waiting for us beneath a summer sky.

SHACKLETON

His journey is over at last, they say,
And his closing trip is done;
But when his body is lifeless clay
The march has only begun;
Down where the southern sea mists roll,
Even the glacier walls
Form no frontier for the restless soul
When the great adventure calls.

Freed from the flesh that fades to dust,
His spirit rides the night,
Wind-blown over the frozen crust
With the southern goal in sight,
Held by the barrier no more
In the crowded inn called Life,
Now a part of the sea-lashed shore
Where the far gales know their strife.

And somewhere he shall meet his mate
By ice pack, wind and foam,
Where the ghost of Scott still battles fate
And brave hearts feel at home.
For "death is a very little thing"
Where lost trails beckon far,
And the unleashed soul at last takes wing
To speed by the final star.